Lands of our Ancestors
Teacher's Guide

Developed by
Cathleen Chilcote Wallace
and Gary Robinson

© 2016 Tribal Eye Productions
P.O. Box 1123 / Santa Ynez, CA 93460
www.tribaleyeproductions.com

TABLE OF CONTENTS

1. Introduction to the Teacher Guide   p. 5

2. Overview of the Chumash People   p. 6

3. The Chumash in Historic Times   p. 7

4. Images of Chumash Traditional Life   p. 8

5. Accuracy of Events Portrayed   p. 11

6. Information Sources on the Chumash People   p. 13

7. Information Sources on California Missions   p. 13

8. Chapter Questions & Answers   p. 14

9. Student Projects   p. 67

Lands of Our Ancestors

Teachers Guide Introduction

This Teachers Guide is designed to enrich teaching Lands of Our Ancestors across the curriculum. The guide begins with an overview of the Chumash people before European contact. This information will provide the teacher with important background information about the Chumash people in pre-Columbian California and can be used to introduce the book. This is followed by a summary of the Chumash in historic times up to the present where the cultural revitalization work of present day Chumash people is also highlighted. In addition, there are three pages of images of traditional Chumash houses, foods, tools, a ceremonial leader, and a hunter. These images help illustrate the story. At this point the guide also includes a section that validates the accuracy of the events portrayed in the story and a list of sources of further information on the Chumash and the historic missions.

The second section of the guide contains "Questions, Answers, and Words to Know" for each chapter of Lands of Our Ancestors. The questions can be used in teacher directed class discussions, small group discussions, or as written work. The variety of questions in each chapter align with The Six Levels of Questioning: knowledge, comprehension, application, analysis, synthesis, evaluation. Answers are provided for all chapter questions. New vocabulary, including Chumash words, are found in each chapter's "Words to Know" page.

Finally, to extend the learning after the book is completed, the guide includes eight project choices to engage students. The projects are designed to meet the needs of the diverse learners found in most classrooms. Each project meets a specific fourth grade History-Social Science Content Standard for California Public Schools. The standard is listed with each project.

Students who complete reading the story, discuss or write responses to the questions, and learn the new vocabulary words will meet a variety of the fourth grade California Common Core State Standards in reading, writing, and language.

Overview of the Chumash People Before European Contact

The Chumash Indians have lived along the south central California coast and nearby inland regions for at least 13,000 years. Their prehistoric territory stretched from Malibu in the south to Morro Bay and San Luis Obispo in the north, and from the Channel Islands in the west to the inland areas around Cuyama, CA. Over time, the language of these autonomous groups evolved into eight different versions of the Chumash language, related to one another in a way similar to how Latin, Italian and Spanish are related to each other.

The Chumash way of life depended on the natural world around them. This world provided everything the people needed for food, clothing, shelter, medicine, tools and weapons. Because they lived so close to nature, the Chumash had very detailed knowledge about the wild plants, animals, and minerals that they relied on.

They knew how to use more than 150 different plants for food, medicine and ceremonial applications. These included oak trees for acorns, chia seeds from sage plants, plus the nuts, seeds, bulbs, roots and leaves of many other plants. However, acorns were *the* most important plant food for the Chumash and most California Indians. Acorns are poisonous to humans unless they are first ground into a fine meal, washed (leached) at least three times and then cooked. This makes a filling, thick brown mush somewhat like oatmeal, often eaten with more flavorful foods like dried fish or venison (deer meat). Pine nuts were also an important food. Trips to pine tree forests at distant higher elevations were part of the Chumash annual food-gathering cycle.

They were skillful hunters of wild games such as deer, antelope, rabbits, birds and seals. They also enjoyed a wide variety of fish and shellfish that came from the ocean and rivers in the area. Salmon of the Santa Ynez River was one of their favorites.

The Chumash home was built of tule reeds spread over frames made of willow branches. This round half-dome house, called an *ap* (op) included a small fire pit at the center with a small smoke hole in the roof. Sizes of these homes varied greatly depending on the size of the family living in one. A village was often made up of rows of aps and included an enclosed area for religious activities, acorn storage facilities, a playing field for sporting games, and a sweat house where daily hot sweat baths were taken for both cleansing and healing.

Their religious beliefs included an understanding of certain supernatural powers that resided in the natural world, including the sky world. Movements of the sun, moon and stars revealed hidden meanings to the tribal spiritual leaders who keep an ever-watchful eye on the sky. These people were part of the twelve-member council called the *antap* (ontop) that provided leadership and guidance to members of the community. Each major village had its own council of twelve, which included the local village chief.

This way of life was developed and practiced for thousands years uninterrupted until the arrival of Spanish priest, soldiers and settlers in the 1700s.

The Chumash in Historic Times

Explorers sailing on Spanish ships visited the California coast a few times in the 1500s and 1600s, but it wasn't until 1769 that Gaspar de Portola led an expedition to the region to establish permanent settlements here. This was a combined religious and military effort to insure that Spain had firm colonial control of the area. Franciscan priests were charged with the duty of creating Catholic missions to convert Indians to Christianity, and soldiers were assigned the duty of maintaining order within these communities. Their ultimate goal was to add more territory to the Spanish empire.

Starting in San Diego, a total of twenty-one missions were established and operated, but these institutions were more like slave plantations than outposts of the Christian faith. Indians who came to the missions were forced to work daily to build all the buildings, raise and slaughter cattle, plant and harvest crops, prepare and cook food, weave cloth for clothing, and perform all the tasks needed to maintain a Spanish settlement. If Indians failed to do their work or tried to run away because of the way they were treated, soldiers on horseback were sent to capture them and bring them back. Then the Indians were often beaten with whips as punishment, or locked in shackles to prevent them from trying again.

Five missions were built in Chumash territory, and due to the spread of European diseases and abusive slave labor practices, the tribal population shrank by at least 80% during the sixty-year mission period. This was true of the Native American population all over the California region.

The Indians that survived did learn domestic skills like how to plant and harvest crops, ride horses, tend cattle, cook European foods, use tools, and wash clothes, but in the years following the end of the mission era, that's all they were allowed to do. They became the underpaid servants of the Mexican landowners who took over the area after Mexico won independence from Spain.

And Indians fared no better under American rule after 1848 when the U.S. took the Southwest from Mexico in war. Congress then declined to ratify treaties with California tribes, and the newly created state government passed laws stripping all rights from indigenous people.

However, today, the Chumash people, particularly the tiny Santa Ynez Band of Chumash, have begun to rebuild their tribal nation. Using revenues from their federally authorized casino and resort, they are providing education and health services to their people. Instruction in tribal history, culture and language are allowing new generations of Chumash to forge a new, hopeful future.

In fact, tribes all over California have been able to begin regaining lost cultures and re-learning nearly lost languages in the 21st century. These losses were directly caused by the priests and soldiers who founded and operated the Spanish missions and were determined to convert California's Native Americans into Spanish colonial citizens at any cost.

Examples of Chumash Traditional Life

Chumash House - Ap (op)

Chumash Village Scene

Examples of Chumash Traditional Life-p.2

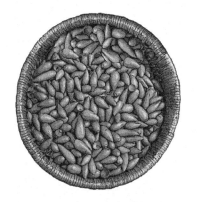

Acorns: A major food for
many California Indians

Acorn grinding stone

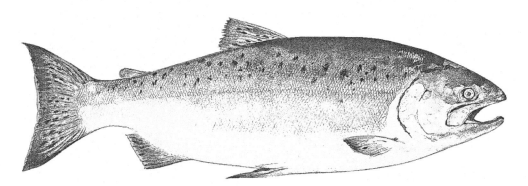

Salmon: an important food
for the Chumash

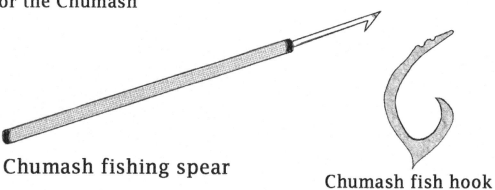

Chumash fishing spear

Chumash fish hook

Examples of Chumash Traditional Life - p.3

Chumash
Ceremonial Leader

Chumash hunter
wearing a deer decoy
head and skin

Accuracy of Events Portrayed in <u>Lands of our Ancestors</u>

As stated in the "Note to Teachers and Parents" at the beginning to <u>Lands of our Ancestors</u>, this work of historical fiction depicts what *might* have happened when a village of Chumash Indian people encountered the Spanish padres and soldiers who came to California to establish religious missions and create colonial outposts in the area. The missions, presidios and settlements they established all relied on forced Indian labor to operate, a fact that has been hidden from public view far too long.

Spanish colonial Franciscan priests, led by Junipero Serra, ultimately forced Indians to build twenty-one of these institutions between San Diego and Sonoma, impacting the lives of at least 100,000 indigenous people from forty or more different tribes. The California Native population was depleted by about 80% as a result of the mission approach to converting Indians not only to Christianity, but also to "civilized" Spanish citizens.

What happens to the Chumash characters in <u>Lands of our Ancestors</u> is typical of what may have happened to all the tribal people who came into contact with any of the missions built on their ancestral lands. The scenes in the book such as the intense flogging of Indians who attempted to escape and depictions of daily schedules and forced labor are soundly rooted in historical research.

The books listed in the bibliography include some of the sources of that historical research. Below is a summary of the research on the punishments used by the priests against Indians who didn't follow mission rules.

Junipero Serra's mandate from the King of Spain was to educate the Indians of California and then release them. Instead, Serra took it upon himself to effectively imprison them for life and use the Native Americans as forced labor… The mission Indians, called neophytes by the friars, had terrible, <u>sadistic punishments</u> inflicted on them by the Franciscans… One distinguished visitor to Mission Carmel was shocked at the fetid <u>squalor</u> in which the Indians were forced to live. Bedraggled Indians, some in <u>shackles</u> and <u>stocks</u>, were being walked to a work site accompanied by guards who swung <u>whips</u> to ensure their staying together. The sight, he wrote in his log, was no different than the slave plantations he'd visited in the Caribbean. He described the policies of the Franciscans toward the mission Indians as *reprehensible, adding they were <u>beating the Indians for violations that in Europe would be considered insignificant</u>.*

By far, one of the cruelest incidents was described in 1825 by Robert Forbes, the master of a New England trading ship. He visited Mission San Francisco and was shocked by the <u>savagery</u> of the friars. He took note of the "Christianizing Padres" who converted the Indians by sending gauchos and rancheros into the field to catch them with a lasso. He said the friars then branded the Indians with a hot branding iron shaped like a cross.

At both Mission San Gabriel and Mission San Luis Rey, the Indians faced the twisted wrath of Friar Jose Zalvidea. A visiting rancher noted the padre's penchant for punishment including his cruelty toward women who suffered miscarriages. Instead of offering comfort, the friar ordered them to be <u>lashed</u> for 15 days, their heads shaved, and <u>irons</u> bolted around their ankles for 3 months. Each bereaved mother also had to stand every Sunday on the steps of the church <u>hold a hideous painted wooden child</u> in her arms.

-Source: <u>A Cross of Thorns</u> by Elias Castillo.

Due to their "animal-like natures," California Indians often made mistakes or misbehaved even when they had been told the rules. Like good fathers everywhere, the padres believed in firm discipline and consequences; usually this meant <u>flogging</u>, but sometimes other kinds of corporal punishment were used. In a long letter of complaint to the King of Spain, one South American Indian provided a <u>catalog of Spanish punishments</u> for Indians that included <u>flogging</u>, <u>hanging upside down</u>, and being <u>put in stocks</u>. Franciscans Fathers used these and other disciplinary actions to help "civilize" California Indians and turn them into good Christians and loyal Spanish subjects. These included those already mentioned plus <u>beating with a cudgel</u>, <u>whipping with a cat-o-nine tails</u> and <u>hobbling with an ankle hobble</u>.

-Source: <u>Bad Indians</u> by Deborah A. Miranda.

Sources on the Chumash People:

1. California's Chumash Indians, A Project of the Santa Barbara Museum of Natural History; EZ Nature Books; 1992, Revised Edition 2002.

2. The Chumash, Seafarers of the Pacific Coast; Karen Bush Gibson; Capstone Press, 2004.

3. "The Samala People" (DVD); produced by the Santa Ynez Band of Chumash Indians; Available from the tribe's Culture Department; 805-688-7997.

4. Bad Indians: A Tribal Memoir; Deborah A. Miranda; Heyday, 2013.

5. Samala-English Dictionary-A Guide to the Samala Language of the Ineseno Chumash People; Santa Ynez Band of Chumash Indians with Richard Applegate, PhD; 2007.

6. Website: www.sbnature.org/research/anthro/chumash/intro.htm (Chumash section of the Santa Barbara Museum of Natural History's website)

7. Website: www.santaynezchumash.org/history.html (The Santa Ynez Band of Chumash Indians official website)

8. Wikipedia Website: https://en.wikipedia.org/wiki/Chumash_people

Sources on California Missions:

1. A Cross of Thorns-The Enslavement of California's Indians by the Spanish Missions; Elias Castillo; Craven Street Books; 2015.

2. Junipero Serra, the Vatican, and Enslavement Theology; Daniel Fogel; Ism Press; 1988.

3. The Other Slavery-The Uncovered Story of Indian Enslavement in America; Andres Resendez; Houghton Mifflin Harcourt; 2016.

4. http:// www.whenturtlesfly.blogspot.com - Deborah Miranda's blog on California Indians and the Native experience in the missions.

5. Website: http://www.missionscalifornia.com; hosted by the California Missions Resource Center. (NOTE: This is a one-sided presentation of facts about the missions and gives no indications that there were negative aspects to mission life for California's Indians.)

6. Website: http://www.huffingtonpost.com/the-zinn-education-project/lying-to-children-about-t_b_6924346.html. (NOTE: This article on the Internet points out the blatant stereotypes found in most material used to teach the "Mission Unit."

Lands of Our Ancestors

Chapter 1
Preparations
Questions

1. Describe the main characters Kilik and Tuhuy. Compare and contrast the boys. What is their relationship?

2. What is the game that Kilik and Tuhuy are playing? Describe the game; how is it played? What is the function of the game and why does Kilik practice with such determination?

3. When the story begins, what time of the year is it? Explain the importance of the season. What do you imagine the mood of the village is?

4. What did you learn about the Chumash people of the Place of River Turtles in Chapter 1? List three facts from the story.

Chapter 1
Answers

1. Kilik is twelve years old. His name means "Sparrow Hawk". He is
    confident, determined, athletic, and a leader. Kilik is eager to use his hunting
    skills to bring food to the village.

    Tuhuy is eleven years old. His name means "Rain". He is a "thinker" and is
    determined to improve his skills although he does not believe he will ever be
    as skilled as Kilik.

    Kilik and Tuhuy are cousins and best friends who are always together. They
    are both kind, obedient, and respectful to their families and elders. They
    work together, each using their special abilities to complete a task or solve a
    problem.

2. Kilik and Tuhuy play the traditional hoop-and-pole game. One boy rolls a
    small hoop on the ground and the other boy throws a long spear-like pole
    through the hoop. The game helps boys develop their hunting skills. Kilik is
    determined to have sharp skills for his first hunt.

3. The story begins at the end of summer. It is the time for Hutash, the yearly
    harvest festival. Hutash is also the name for Mother Earth.
    The mood in the village is probably excited, busy, and thoughtful.
    (Accept other appropriate responses.)

4. Facts from Chapter 1 about the Chumash people:
    *   The Chumash people live in villages, in homes made of tule reeds,
        with leaders and extended family members.
    *   Family groups work together and help each other.
    *   The Chumash people (and all native people) respect Mother Earth.
    *   Chumash children are expected to work but also play games and have
        toys.
    *   Traditions are important to the Chumash people.
    *   Dances, songs, and stories are important to the Chumash culture.
    *   (Accept other appropriate answers.)

Chapter 1
Words to Know

Chumash Names and Words:

Kilik (Kee-leek): Sparrow Hawk; young boy
Tuhuy (Too-hooy): Rain; young boy, Kilik's cousin
Salapay (Sal-uh-pie): To lift or raise up; Tuhuy's father, Kilik's uncle
Solomol (Soh-loh-mole): To straighten and arrow; Kilik's father, Tuhuy's uncle
Wonono (Wo-no-no): Small Owl; Kilik's mother
Yol (rhymes with pole): Bluebird; Tuhuy's mother
Stuk (Rhymes with Luke): Ladybug; Kilik's sister
Kimi (Kee-mee): To repeat, do over; Stuk's nickname

Hutash: Chumash harvest ceremony; Chumash name for Mother Earth

Chumash: The Chumash are native people of the south-central region of California who have lived in the area for at least 9,000 years. The people lived in small self-governing groups spread over several thousand square miles. Different Chumash languages were spoken in the communities. In this book, the tribe lives in the Santa Ynez Valley and speaks Samala Chumash. Other Chumash groups are known as Barbareño and Ventureño.

Words to Know
(in order of appearance in the story)

ancestor: a person related to you who lived a long time ago; your grandmother's grandmother and anyone who lived before her

hurl: to throw with great force

thrust: to push something suddenly in a specific direction

cease: stop, quit, discontinue

quiver: a case for holding arrows, usually made from animal skin

Chapter 1
Words to Know

endurance: the ability to keep doing something difficult, unpleasant, or painful for a long time

ceremony: an event with special traditions, actions, or word

harvest: a season when food is gathered from the land

gathering: a time when people come together as a group, especially for a festive occasion

tule reeds: tall, green reeds with spongy stems

acorn granary: a very large, round basket-like receptacle made from willow to store acorns

scornful: a very strong feeling of no respect for someone

tradition: a way of behaving or a belief that has been established for a long time

shell bead money: strands of beads made from small disks shaped from the Olivella shell

trickster: someone who uses their intelligence to play tricks on others and sometimes breaks the rules

Chapter 2
House of the Moon
Questions

1. The day of Kilik's first hunting trip finally arrives. Explain why this is such an important event for him. Can you imagine how he feels as he sets out with his father?

2. In addition to hunting skills, what does Kilik's father teach him? Why do you think this is important?

3. Using evidence (information) from the story, describe the area where the tribe's village is built. Can you think of a reason why the village is built in that location?

4. How would you describe the special relationship the Chumash people (all native people) have with Mother Earth?

5. The double halos around the moon are an example of foreshadowing. What change do you think is coming for the Chumash? Support your prediction with evidence from the story.

Chapter 2
Answers

1. Kilik's first hunting trip is important to him because he wants to prove that he can provide food for his village. Kilik is excited, happy, and maybe nervous on the day of his first hunt. (Accept any appropriate answers.)

2. Kilik's father teaches him the important landmarks, trails, place names, and geography of the area. Kilik needs to know this information because one day he will hunt alone and he needs understand the land.

3. The village is built in a valley on a raised flat area overlooking the river. There are mountains surrounding the valley. The village was built in that area because there is water and good hunting and gathering areas nearby. (Accept any other appropriate answers.)

4. The Chumash people (and all native people) have a great respect and love for Mother Earth. They recognize that the land, plants, animals, and water are the resources they need to survive so they are careful with their environment. Food, clothing, tools, medicine, baskets, housing materials are made from natural resources. (Accept any additional appropriate answers.)

5. The double halos predict a drastic change in the lives of the Chumash people. Evidence from the story: A hunter tells Solomol that strange people wearing odd clothing and speaking an odd language who seem to have more powers than the Chumash leaders have been seen on the lands of the Chumash as well as to the south. These strange people are Spanish soldiers and priests who have come to take the land of the Chumash people.

Chapter 2
Words to Know
(in order of appearance in the story)

Chumash word: haku: hello

talisman: an object that is believed to have magical power and will bring good luck to the person who wears it

nocking: to put the notch in the end of an arrow on the bowstring

carcass: the dead body of an animal

scan: to look carefully, especially in search of something

generation: people born and living at the same time

foothills: low hills at the base of a mountain or mountain range

makeshift: temporary

projectile: any object thrown into space by force

halo: a glowing light that circles something

Chapter 3
The Strangers
Questions

1. How would you describe Solomol and Kilik's preparations to hunt? Compare and contrast the differences in their camouflage. What large animals are they hunting?

2. Explain what Solomol does after Kilik kills the deer.

3. What is your definition of courage? How does Solomon define courage to Kilik?

4. How do you imagine Kilik is feeling after his first successful hunt and his discussion with Solomol? Explain your answer.

5. What conclusions can you draw about the strange visitors who arrive in the village during Hutash? Who are the visitors? What language do they speak? How do the people of the village react to their first meeting?

Chapter 3
Answers

1. Solomol and Kilik begin the day of the hunt in a traditional and respectful way; they say a prayer to Grandfather Sun.
   Solomol and Kilik camouflage themselves so they can move as close to their prey as possible without being noticed by the animal. Solomol wears a deerskin on his back and a dried deer head and antlers tied under his chin with cordage or a strip of leather. Kilik only wears a deerskin covering his back and shoulders. He isn't experienced enough to balance the weight of the deer head and antlers yet.
   Solomol and Kilik are hunting deer and antelope. (Inform students that California native people did not hunt buffalo. The buffalo are not indigenous to California.)

2. After Kilik's arrow kills the deer, Solomol does the following:
   - Showing respect for the deer, Solomol places his hand on the deer's head and says a prayer thanking the deer for the food he will provide to the people in the village.
   - Solomol tells Kilik that he has crossed into manhood and is proud of him.
   - Solomol gives Kilik the talisman necklace that he was given by his own father on his first hunt.
   - Solomol tells Kilik that his skills may be one day needed for more than hunting. He might have to protect his family from enemies.

3. Answers will vary for individual courage definitions.
   Solomon's definition of courage: "Courage comes from within you by joining your mind to your heart." When necessary, your courage will rise up to protect loved ones, even if you are afraid.

4. Individual student answers may vary. Possible responses:
   Kilik is happy and proud of his accomplishments and pleased that his father is proud of him. He is excited to receive the talisman necklace; a sign of tradition being passed on to the next generation. Kilik is suddenly unsure of himself when his father explains that as a man, he will have responsibilities in addition to hunting.

Chapter 3
Answers

5. The visitors who arrive in the village during Hutash are Spanish soldiers and priests sent to build outposts for Spain. They believe all indigenous people are inferior human beings and need to be educated and civilized in the European way. (Text) They speak Spanish and use an Indian translator to help them communicate with the Chumash and possibly to gain their trust. (Inference) To help put the natives at ease, the translator says that the visitors want to make life better for the Chumash. (Text) The visitors immediately try to show their power by using "fire sticks" (guns), unknown to the native people, to impress and frighten them. (Example from text: Soldier shoots the gourds and shocks everyone.) The visitors make it known that they have more "power" than the Indians (Interpreter says that fire-sticks are better than bows and arrows.). The visitors say they will share their knowledge with the Chumash people if they agree to visit their camp. (Example from text: Interpreter's statement, "Come share food. See more powers. Learn truth of their knowledge.") The visitors are using tricks and fear to convince the Indians in the village to visit the camp. (Conclusion)

The Chumash people are friendly, curious, cautious, confused, and afraid. They have many opinions about what the strangers' visit means. (Example from text: The Twelve leaders' debate.)

Chapter 3
Words to Know
(in order of appearance in the story)

shrine: a holy or sacred place

camouflage: a way of hiding people or objects by making them look like the natural background.

doe: a female deer

buck: a male deer

sacrifice: to give up something valuable to help another person

threshold: beginning something new

overcome: to succeed in dealing with a problem or difficulty

venison: meat from a deer

envious: wanting to have what someone else has

bounty: a variety and generous amount of food

indigenous: a person, plant, or animal native to an area

tongue: language

interpreter: someone who translates between languages

proclaim: to announce or declare officially or publicly

gourd: a fruit with a hard outer shell that is used to make rattles for music and containers for food and water

Chapter 3
Words to Know

dismay: worry, disappointment, upset

awe: a strong feeling of respect sometimes mixed with fear or surprise

debate: to discuss, argue, dispute

timid: shy, fearful, lacking confidence

Chapter 4
Buzzard Food
Questions

1. How many people are chosen to travel to the strangers' camp and who makes the decision? What evidence can you find that shows the chief does not trust the strangers? Do you agree with his reasoning? Explain your answer.

2. Describe what Kilik and Tuhuy see when they arrive at the strangers' camp. In your opinion, how might the characters feel at first?

3. How would you describe the language problems Kilik and his family find in the camp? How does this problem help the priests and soldiers? What can you conclude about the native languages in California?

4. What evidence from the text justifies the conclusion that the native people already living in the camp when Kilik arrives are treated poorly?

5. What facts or ideas show that the behavior of the priests and soldiers do not change when Kilik and his family arrive? What is it that the people of the Place of the River Turtles do not realize at the end of the first day of their visit?

Chapter 4
Answers

1. The chief of the Place of the River Turtles chooses about fifty people to travel to the strangers' camp. The chief chooses the best village protectors to make the journey. He tells the men to take their bows and arrows and to be ready to defend the people. This evidence shows that the chief does not trust the strangers.
   Accept reasonable responses with supporting evidence for student opinion.

2. When Kilik and Tuhuy arrive, they see:
   - oak trees that have been cut down (Acorn gathered from the oak trees are important food for the native people.)
   - cattle (Animals unknown to the native people.)
   - adobe buildings and adobe brick making (European style buildings)
   - native people looking sad and tired and guarded by soldiers
   - strange food
   - natives plowing the fields

   The characters may feel overwhelmed, curious, confused, or afraid.
   Accept reasonable responses for student opinion.

3. Kilik and his family do not understand the language spoken by the priests and soldiers. They also do not understand the languages of the other native people living at the camp. This is an advantage to the priests and soldiers because the native people are unaware of what is being said around them. Since communication among the native people is difficult, they remain isolated. This helps the priests and soldiers control the native people.
   Student conclusion: There are many diverse California native languages.

4. Evidence from the text that the native people already living in the camp are treated poorly:
   - native people are given poor quality food
   - native people appear skinny, tired, sad
   - native people spend the days doing hard work
   - native people are always guarded by soldiers

Chapter 4
Answers

5. The priests and soldiers continue to try to convince the native people that they will learn new skills, their lives will improve, they (the priests) only want the best for the native people, and they will be paid for their work. When the native people appear to want to leave, the priests show them beads; a bribe to stay. Also, the soldiers surround the native people to keep them in the camp. The people of the Place of the River Turtles are unaware that when they entered the camp, they will be captive; unable to leave.

Chapter 4
Words to Know
(in order of appearance in the story)

prattle: to talk for a long time

stocky: sturdy, chunky

acorn: rounded nut from an oak tree

salmon: a large edible fish with red or pink flesh

buzzard: a large hawk-like bird of prey with broad wings and a rounded tail

intention: plan, purpose

Chapter 5
What's Going On Here?
Questions

1. Why do you think the Chumash people are separated on their first night in the camp? What reason does the interpreter give? Do you believe him? Why or why not?

2. Can you explain what is happening when the soldier insists that Kilik and Tuhuy wear the garments?

3. What motivates the soldiers to remove the men's bows, arrows, and spears while they sleep? Why do you think Solomol and Salapay do not continue to protest? What is the priest's message that the translator gives the men?

4. The translator tells Kilik's group, "Today you be blessed to begin new life. Leave savage ways behind and receive a new name." Explain what happens next, Kilik's reaction, and the outcome. Do you agree with the actions of the priests and soldiers? Why or why not?

5. What do Kilik, Solomol, and Salapay finally realize on the second morning in camp?

Chapter 5
Answers

1. The Chumash people are separated on their first night in the camp to begin to break down the family groups. This gives the priests and soldiers control and prevents the native people from leaving if family members are in unknown locations in the camp. (Accept additional reasonable answers.) The interpreter tells the people that if they are separated, it will be easier to protect them and keep track of. ("Make sure all are where they belong.") Opinions on the interpreter's comment will vary.

2. The soldiers and priests have no respect or understanding of the Chumash culture or traditions. The soldier is insisting that Kilik and Tuhuy wear the garments because dressing in the European way is the beginning of changing how the natives live. The soldier knocks Kilik down to show his control over the boys and to instill fear so they won't fight back or object.

3. The soldiers remove the native men's bows, arrows, and spears while they sleep so that the men will be helpless; unable to fight or escape. Solomol and Salapay do not continue to protest because the soldiers are pointing their "fire-sticks" at the men's heads. The priest's message that the translator tells the men is: "Man-in-sky has delivered you to us. And here you and our people will stay." He informs the men that they will not leave the camp.

4. After the translator says, "Today you be blessed to begin new life. Leave savage ways behind and receive a new name." the priest begins to baptize and rename the native people in Kilik's village. The priest gives the native people Spanish names and baptizes them into a new religion. The people are required to be renamed and baptized; to become European. Kilik objects; he does not want a new name and does not want to join the camp community. However, the soldiers force the native people to undergo the process with force if necessary. The soldier makes an example out of Kilik by shooting his gun near Kilik's head, drawing everyone's attention, forcing him to comply. Then he pushes Kilik, who trips and falls. This renaming and baptizing procedure is a step toward taking away the Chumash culture, tradition, and individual identity.
Accept appropriate student opinion responses.

5. In the morning, Kilik, Solomol, and Salapay finally realize that they will not be leaving the camp. They are not guests; they are captives.

Chapter 5
Words to Know
(in order of appearance in the story)

garment: an item of clothing

adequate: enough, suitable, satisfactory

gibberish: nonsense, meaningless speech

trudge: a long, slow, difficult walk

savage: people considered to be primitive and uncivilized

escort: to guide, lead

Chapter 6
Coyote Men
Questions

1. What is the main idea of Chapter 6?

2. What is the "loud clanging sound" and what is its purpose? (Use clues from the story.) How are the "loud clanging sounds" and the strange food related to controlling the native people?

3. Describe the job Kilik and Tuhuy are given and its importance.

4. What advice does the translator give to Kilik and Tuhuy? What warning does he give them?

Chapter 6
Answers

1. The main idea of Chapter 6: Although the priests promise a new life, the priests and soldiers use force and brutality to make Chumash people of the Place of the River Turtles become slaves of the Spanish mission system.

2. The loud clanging sound is made by bells in the camp. The lives of the native people in the camp are regulated by the ringing of the bells; they must follow the schedule of the bells. The bells keep the people moving from task to task in a regimented way; lining up, waiting, working, eating, sleeping. This makes them easier to guard. The strange food keeps the native people hungry, poorly nourished, and tired. Tired, hungry people are less likely to fight the soldiers or try to escape.

3. Kilik and Tuhuy are assigned jobs making adobe bricks. (This job existed in all of the missions.) The bricks are used to make the European style buildings. The bricks are made by mixing water, dirt, and dried grass together. The mixture is placed into a wooden frame and dried in the sun. The brick is later removed from the frame. Kilik and Tuuy haul water from the river for brick making. It is hard work to make the bricks and a large supply is necessary for making the buildings of the new Mission.

4. Advice given to Kilik and Tuhuy by the translator:
   - Don't mention Chumash names in front of the priests; there will be punishment.
   - Keep busy and there won't be trouble.

   Warning given to Kilik and Tuhuy by the translator:
   - Don't try to run away, you will be captured, brought back, and punished.

Words to Know
Chapter 6
(in order of appearance in the story)

usher: to show or guide someone somewhere

brisk: fast, quick

drone: to go on and on talking in a dull tone

adobe: a sun dried brick made from a mixture of dirt, water, and dried grass

Chapter 7
The Bells
Questions

1. In your opinion, what are four of the biggest adjustments the Chumash people are required to make in their daily lives?

2. The Chumash people did not dare contradict or question the padres directly. Do you agree with this decision? Why or why not?
   When did Kilik and his family have an opportunity to quietly break the rules? Why was this important?

3. List some of the jobs the native people must do at the mission. Do men and women work at the same jobs? What must both men and women do daily?

4. The padres' strict rules have punishments. Describe what the padres believe about the Indians and punishment. What offences are punished? What are the punishments?

5. Kilik, Solomol, and Salapay have specific concerns or worries. How would you describe and evaluate their concerns?

Chapter 7
Answers

1. Four of the biggest adjustments the Chumash people are required to make:
   - Language; must learn Spanish, not allowed to speak native language
   - Religion; must learn Catholic religion
   - Separated from family members
   - Hard physical work
   - Insufficient food
   - Illness
   - Fear of punishment

   Accept any additional reasonable answers.

2. Student opinion replies will vary as to why the Chumash people did not dare to contradict or question the padres, but should include fear of severe punishment and the human will to survive.
   Kilik and his family quietly break the rules at mealtime at the mission. This is important because it is an opportunity to speak their native language, remember who they are, where they come from, and to keep hope alive.

3. Men and women work at separate jobs in the mission.
   Men's jobs: brick making, building construction, field work, planting, harvesting, cattle/animal care, blacksmith work

   Women's jobs: laundry, weaving cloth, cooking, cleaning, working in vegetable gardens

   Men and women are required to study the Bible and learn to speak Spanish.

4. The padres think the Indians are children and they must have physical punishment when they break the rules. The padres believe this is the only way they will learn.
   Offenses: speaking native language, not working, meeting friends, escaping, contradicting the padres or soldiers
   Punishments: include whipping, stocks, hobbling feet, washing mouth with soap, hitting, pushing, capture

Chapter 7
Answers

5. Solomol and Salapay are concerned that the others from their village will look for them and also become captive. They don't want anyone else from their village to be taken.

   Kilik is worried about the changes he sees in his sister, Stuk's, behavior. She has changed from talkative, outgoing, and curious to withdrawn and quiet. (This is symbolic of the effect of the harsh treatment the Indians received at all of the missions; resulting in a loss of hope and spirit.)

Chapter 7
Words to Know
(in order of appearance in the story)

padre: Spanish word for priest

contradict: challenge, argue against, deny

loom: a tool for weaving threads into cloth

stocks: feet and ankles are locked into the device and legs held out straight; used as a harsh punishment

hobble: to tie a strap around the feet to make walking difficult; used as a harsh punishment

Chapter 8
The Secret Plan
Questions

1. Who are the "trustees"? What is their purpose? How do the padres motivate the trustees?

2. Why do Salapay and Solomol plan an escape? What is the result? How might it have ended differently?

3. The brutal punishment that Slomol and Salapay receive is a consequence of their escape plan. What other purpose does the punishment serve? Use evidence from the story to support your answer.

4. What judgment would you make about Father Espíritu? Support your comments with examples from the story.

5. What advantages do Kilik and Tuhuy have when they begin working as Father Espíritu's assistants? What important information do they learn?

Chapter 8 Answers

1. The trustees are Indians who have been at the mission for a long time and speak Spanish well. The padres choose them. The trustees make sure the Indians are following the rules and report any problems or rule breaking to the padres and soldiers.
   If the trustee does not do his job, he and his family will be punished.

2. Solomol and Salapay decide to plan an escape because they realize what a horrible place the mission is and they want to protect their families and people. The plan is ruined by a trustee, Reynaldo, who reports them to the soldiers.
   Answers for how the situation might have ended differently will vary.

3. The flogging of Solomol and Slapay serves to physically hurt and punish the men for their escape plan. It also makes an example of them to the other native people; discouraging others from trying to escape. This breaks down the hope of the people and reinforces fear of the soldiers and trustees. By allowing the trustee to participate in the flogging, a separation and lack of trust develops between the native people.

4. Opinions about Father Espíritu will vary but should be supported by examples from the text. Father Espíritu wants to covert the Indians but feels they should not be harshly punished. He is a much kinder man than Father Fiero. Examples from text:
   * Father Espíritu thinks Father Fiero treats the Indians too cruelly, he confronts Father Fiero and says he will write a complaint letter to the head of the Missions in Mexico City.
   * When Salapay and Solomol are flogged, Father Espíritu wants to give them medicine for their wounds, but Father Fiero won't let him.
   * Father Espíritu feels sorry for Kilik's and Tuhuy's fathers and offers them jobs as his assistants. He admits to them that he feels Father Fiero's punishments are too harsh.

5. When Kilik and Tuhuy begin working for Father Espíritu, they no longer have to do the hard work of making adobe bricks or working in the fields in the hot sun. They also have the opportunity to overhear conversations between the priests and gather information to share with other native people in the mission. Kilik and Tuhuy learn that originally the native people would be released from the Mission when they became "civilized".

Chapter 8
Words to Know
(in order of appearance in the story)

trustee: a person who works for those in charge and makes sure rules are followed

incentive: something that encourages a person to do something

cohesive: when parts fit together, united

co-conspirators: people involved in a secret plan

flog: to beat someone with a whip or stick as a punishment or torture

mete: give out carefully

civilized: a high level of social, cultural, and technological development

Chapter 9
A Small Vacation
Questions

1. What conclusions can you make about the effects of the flogging on the native people living at the mission?

2. Compare and contrast the motives of Father Espíritu, Father Fiero, and Captain Castigar regarding "the small vacation".

3. List two ways the soldiers were disrespectful to the Indians during the day away from the mission.

4. Explain the information the village elder tells Solomol and Salapay when the group visits their home, Place of the River Turtles.

5. What information does the visit to the village give you about the effect of the missions on native people left behind in the villages?

Chapter 9
Answers

1. The flogging upsets and depresses the other native people in the mission. They don't want to work as hard as they did before even when they are punished. They feel helpless, resentful, and probably hate the priests and soldiers more than before.
   A consequence of the flogging for the priests is lower production of goods made at the mission. This results in less money earned for the mission.

2. Father Espíritu is sympathetic to the Indians. He feels sorry for them after the flogging and wants to raise their spirits.
   Father Fiero wants the Indians to start working and producing again. He is convinced by Father Espíritu that the day away from the mission will help.
   Captain Castigar wants to show the native people that their village is abandoned and they don't have homes to return to. This reinforces his control over the Indians and their feeling of helplessness.

3. The soldiers are disrespectful to the Indians on the day of their trip away from the mission in these ways:
   - The soldiers eat and gorge themselves on the gathered and cooked food prepared by the Indian women. The Indians must eat whatever is left.
   - Captain Castigar and the soldiers do not learn the Chumash language. Captain Castigar refers to the native language as "gibberish".
   - When the Chumash visit their village, Captain Castigar is "smug" and seems happy to see the village in ruins and abandoned.
   - The village elder they meet is left without food or help.

4. The village elder tells Solomol and Salapay that the Indians who have escaped from the missions are hiding at the base of Sacred Mountain.

5. The missions had an effect on all the native people, those taken captive and those left behind. People not taken to the mission were often the old ones. They were unable to provide for themselves left alone in the village. These people became sick, starved, and died. Those who escaped the missions had to stay in hiding so that they wouldn't be captured; they were not completely free.

Chapter 9
Words to Know
(in order of appearance in the story)

witnessing: to see, watch, observe

escort: to lead

flee: to run away

snare: a type of woven trap

edible: safe to eat, can be eaten

skewer: a long piece of wood used for holding food together while cooking

gorge: eat greedily, fill up fast

eerily: strange, creepy

linger: to stay back

Chapter 10
Is All Hope Lost?
Questions

1. Two years pass as captives in the mission for Kilik and his family. Summarize what this means for the priests and soldiers. Explain what it means for the native people. Use evidence from the story.

2. What conditions at the mission contribute to the high death rate among the native people? What statements in the chapter prove that the priests do not care about the Indians?

3. How would you describe the relationship between Kilik and Tuhuy after two years at the mission?

4. Discuss what some of the Chumash leaders do secretly and its importance.

5. At this point in the story, if you could speak to one of the native people living in the mission, what would you say?

Chapter 10
Answers

1. After two years, the mission's buildings are completed, crops, cattle, and products for sale and trade are being made. Indians are converted to the Catholic religion and are being "civilized". Even if by force, this all means success for the priests and soldiers. They are meeting their goals.
For the Indians, the passage of time means a loss of physical and mental health, happiness, family, language, and culture. They are slaves living in the mission facing daily punishment. (Evidence from the text should be included.)

2. Conditions at the mission that contribute to the high death rate among the native people are: difficult and harsh working conditions, poor diets, severe physical punishment, untreated injuries, illness, and disease.

   Statements in the chapter that prove the priests' lack of concern for the native people:
   - "Most of those who died were unceremoniously placed in unmarked graves." (This occurred throughout the mission system.)
   - "…a padre marked down the name of the deceased and the date of his death in a big book, but that was all." (Record keeping)
   - "…these departed Indians were gone and forgotten by the Spaniards."

3. The relationship between Kilik and Tuhuy remains close and strong. Their shared difficult experiences have perhaps made their bond stronger. They continue to support and protect each other. They help each other stay positive and make games out of their work to avoid boredom. (Students may have additional comments and insights.)

4. The Chumash leaders continue to speak their language and mark traditional cycles of time the Chumash way. They are preserving the Chumash culture for future generations.

5. Student responses will vary.

Chapter 10
Words to Know
(in order of appearance in the story)

Advent: a period starting four Sundays before Christmas

Ash Wednesday: for Christians, first day of Lent, 46 days before Easter

Day of Ascension: Catholic celebration 40 days after Easter

Pentecost: a Christian feast on the seventh Sunday after Easter

coincided: to occur at the same time

Winter Solstice: shortest day of the year marking the beginning of winter

Summer Solstice: longest day of the year marking the beginning of summer

drudgery: hard or dull work

hoist: to raise something with ropes or pulleys

unceremoniously: informally, abruptly, rudely

Chapter 11
News Spreads
Questions

1. What is the importance of the Spanish expedition?

2. Why do the priests and soldiers keep the news about the revolts at the other missions a secret?

3. What statement does Salapay make that illustrates the Indians are always being watched and are never safe?

4. Do you agree with Solomol's and Salapay's decision to lead a revolt? Explain your reasoning.

Chapter 11
Answers

1. The Spanish expedition brings supplies, mail, and news from other missions. The expedition leaves with hides, grains, and other items produced by the Indians for export.

2. The Spaniards keep the information about the revolts a secret because they don't want the Indians in their mission to decide to revolt as well. They don't want the Indians to think it's possible to revolt.

3. Salapay's statement: "Even the walls of the mission buildings seem to have ears."

4. Student opinions will vary.

Chapter 11
Words to Know
(in order of appearance in the story)

expedition: a journey by a group of people with a specific purpose

export: to ship goods to another country for sale

revolt: to fight against the rule of a leader or government

rebellion: to rise up and fight those in power

squelch: to put an end to something such as an argument

embolden: to give courage or confidence

urgency: requiring immediate, quick action

quell: to put an end to something

allies: people or groups in agreement; working together toward a common goal

pledge: promise

Chapter 12
The Countdown Begins
Questions

1. How do Indians pass messages between the missions? Why do you think the priests and soldiers are not aware of what the Indians are doing? What message is delivered to Solomol's group?

2. When will the attack happen? How long do the Indians have to prepare?

3. What does Solomol say his reason for fighting is? Do you think Solomol is confident that the revolt will be successful? Explain your answer.

4. What evidence shows that Father Espíritu knows a revolt is going to happen?

Chapter 12
Answers

1. Messages are passed between the missions by the Indians who travel with the expeditions. The visiting Indians from the expeditions eat and sleep with the mission Indians and have opportunities to share information.

   Possible response: The priests and soldiers don't realize what the Indians are doing because they may underestimate the Indians' knowledge of what is happening, they think the Indians are ignorant and uninformed, they may think the soldiers are guarding the Indians well enough to keep them from communicating. (Student opinions will vary, statements should be supported with evidence from the story.)

   Solomol learns from the Indians in the expedition that native people who have escaped other missions and live nearby plan an attack on the mission.

2. The attack will occur on the Summer Solstice, in the early morning while the soldiers are eating breakfast. The Indians living in the mission have one week to prepare.

3. Solomol's reason for fighting is to provide a successful escape for the children. He realizes that in order for the Chumash people to survive, the children must escape.
   Solomol is not confident that the revolt will be successful. He says, "IF the rebellion fails, the future of the Chumash people is the younger generation." He is also aware that the soldiers' weapons are more powerful that the Indians' bows and arrows. (Accept additional reasonable replies.)

4. Father Espíritu gives medical supplies and a burlap bag of "traveling food" to Kilik and Tuhuy. He also tells the boys that he doesn't approve of the treatment of the Indians at the mission.

Chapter 12
Words to Know
(in order of appearance in the story)

quarters: shelter, house

overheard: to hear what other people are saying without them knowing

inspire: to make someone feel that they want to do something

agonize: to worry

capable: able to do something

chapel: a small church

burlap: a rough cloth made from jute or hemp and used mostly for bags

dorm (dormitory): a large room for sleeping

pine nuts: the edible seed of pine trees

chia seeds: seeds used as food from a native plant

Chapter 13
Summer Solstice
Questions

1. Describe the events and mood in the mission on the morning of the Summer Solstice?

2. Why did Father Espíritu choose to help Kilik, Tuhuy, and the native children? What does he do? In your opinion, is Father Espíritu a brave man? Explain.

3. How would you change or modify the action in the chapter to improve the natives' situation as the fighting begins?

4. Imagine you are in the chapel with Kilik and Tuhuy and the native children, what would you be thinking and feeling?

Chapter 13
Answers

1. Events on the morning of the Summer Solstice:
   - The Indians take weapons from storage room and hide them.
   - Attacking Indians charge the mission.
   - Children led by Kilik and Tuhuy run to safety in the chapel.
   - Reynaldo is sent to the Presidio for help for the soldiers.
   - The fighting begins between the soldiers and Indians.

   The mood in the mission that morning is tense, anxious, fearful, angry, and possibly hopeful. (Answers will vary. Accept reasonable replies.)

2. Father Espíritu unlocks the doors to the chapel so that Kilik, Tuhuy, and the children can go inside and be safe. He tells Kilik that he is helping because he doesn't agree with the Church's treatment of the Indians. He seems to care about the children.

   Father Espíritu risks being found out by the other priests and soldiers. He can be considered brave for putting the well-being of the native children over his own safety and reputation. (Opinions may vary.)

   (During the time of the missions, priests who openly objected to the treatment of the Indians were sent back to Mexico City or other locations.)

3. Students' suggestions to modify the chapter will vary.

4. Accept reasonable, thoughtful replies.

Chapter 13
Words to Know
(in order of appearance in the story)

nocturnal: active at night

stern: strict, serious

rendezvous: meet at agreed time and place

cot: a portable or folding bed

unison: at the same time, together

massive: large and heavy or solid

retreat: moving back or to withdraw

barricade: to block something so that people or things cannot enter or leave

presidio: a military post

sanctuary: a place of safety

Chapter 14
A Near Miss
Questions

1. What role do Kilik and Tuhuy have in the revolt?

2. Can you predict what would have happened if Father Espíritu had not been waiting at the chapel with the keys to the door?

3. How do Kilik and Tuhuy continue to work together and use their special skills to keep the native children safe in the chapel?

4. If you could speak to Solomol and Salapay on the afternoon of the revolt, what would you tell them?

Chapter 14
Answers

1. Kilik and Tuhuy are in charge of taking the native children to the chapel and keeping them hidden and safe during the fighting.

2. Answers will vary.

3. Kilik uses his coordination and running skills to retrieve the burlap bag of food for the children. Tuhuy uses his problem solving skills (thinking skills) to devise a lock for the chapel doors.

4. Accept reasonable answers.

Chapter 14
Words to Know
(in order of appearance in story)

retrieve: to get or bring

frantic: fear, anxiety

courtyard: an open space surrounded by walls or buildings

plaza: an open public space

eruption: an outburst or explosion

crossfire: gunfire from two or more directions passing through the same area

vertical: in an up-down position, upright, at right angles to the horizon

Chapter 15
Call of Duty
Questions

1. What surprise exists in the chapel and how do you think it might be important to Kilik, Tuhuy, and the children?

2. What great responsibility do Kilik and Tuhuy accept? Why must they do this alone? Do you think they will be successful?

3. List the skills and character traits Kilik needs for a successful escape.

4. If Solomol and Salapay know about the trap door in the chapel and the secret door on the mission wall, why do you suppose they don't just take their own families and escape?

Chapter 15
Answers

1. A trap door is in the floor of the chapel behind the altar. It leads down a passage and to a secret door in the mission wall. The trap door can be an escape route for the children.

2. Kilik and Tuhuy must escape with the group of native children and find their way to the village of runaway natives at the base of Sacred Mountain.
   The adults will stay at the mission and fight, causing a distraction while the children escape. All of the Indians trying to escape at once will be too obvious; a large group will move slowly and be too easy to track by the soldiers. Children escaping might not be noticed.
   Students' opinions on the success of the escape will vary.

3. Kilik must rely on his knowledge of the geography of the land and how to move or travel without being seen. (As when tracking animals.) He needs to use his knowledge of the four directions. Kilik must use his hunting skills, knowledge of plants, fire making, and shelter building to feed and protect the children. Kilik must also rely on his courage, determination, and sense of duty that his father said he would have when needed.

4. Opinions why Solomol and Salapay don't make use of the trap door for an escape for themselves and their families leaving the others behind will vary, but should include loyalty, honor, duty.

Chapter 15
Words to Know
(in order of appearance in the story)

altar: a raised platform in a church where ceremonies are performed

engulf: to completely surround or cover

hobbling: to walk in an awkward way usually due to injury

volley: a burst or outpouring of many things at once

dawn: the first appearance of light in the sky before sunrise

Chapter 16
The Final Escape
Questions

1. After leaving the mission, what obstacles do Kilik, Tuhuy, and the native children encounter?

2. How is an understanding of nature related to a successful escape for Kilik's group?

3. Can you predict the outcome of the escape and journey of Kilik, Tuhuy, and the native children? What do you think will happen to the native people in the mission?

4. What makes the event in this story important in California history? Use information from the story and your unit of study to explain your answer.

Chapter 16
Answers

1. After leaving the mission, the obstacles Kilik, Tuhuy, and the native children meet are: difficult, slow walking off the trails, rain, hunger, fear of capture by soldiers, fatigue, cold, and broken down shelters for sleeping.
   (Accept other reasonable answers.)

2. An understanding of nature is essential to a successful escape for Kilik, Tuhuy, and the children. Kilik knows how to follow the animal trails for safety and how to use the tall grass to hide in. He recognizes landmarks such as Mother Oak to guide their way. Kilik uses the sounds of the horses' hooves and the flock of birds as warnings to hide. He knows what resources to use to make fire and find food. He understands to find his direction to travel, he must go to a high point (Shrine Mountain).

3. Predictions and opinions of the outcome of the escape and what will happen to those left at the mission will vary. Encourage students to use previous knowledge about mission history to make reasonable predictions and to support opinions.

4. Opinions on the importance of the event in the story in California history will vary. Answers may include: Spanish land acquisition by force, coerced religious conversion, destruction of native culture and languages, drastic decrease in native populations, change in environment due to introduction of non-native plants and animals.

Chapter 16
Words to Know
(in order of appearance in the story)

pews: long benches with a back used to sit on in churches

mourning doves: a bird; a dove with a long tail, gray-brown back, sad call

beacon: a light set up high to guide, warn, or signal

expose: uncovered, unprotected

flock (birds): group of birds

roosting: birds resting, sleeping

retreat: withdraw from enemy, moving back

dedication: committed to a task or purpose

contemplate: to think about

foretelling: to predict

gratitude: thankfulness

Lands of Our Ancestors
Projects

The following suggested projects and activities will extend the learning of early California history across the curriculum. Each project meets at least one of the fourth grade History-Social Science Content Standards in section 4.2:

"Students describe the social, political, cultural, and economic life and interactions among people of California from the pre-Columbian societies to the Spanish mission and Mexican rancho periods."

The projects are appropriate for individual students, partners, or small groups. Completed projects can be presented to the entire class for shared learning. All materials needed for the projects are basic classroom and school supplies. Laptops, notebooks, and the school library are resources the students will also need.

Projects and Activities

History Through Storytelling (Standard 4.2.1)

Storytelling is an important element of native culture. The stories carry a tribe's (and a family's) history, teach lessons about how people should behave, explain how things came to be in the world, and teach how to care for the land and animals.

Group Project: The students will choose a California Native American story that interests them.
- The students should identify the origin of the story; Chumash, Tongva, Yokut, Ohlone, or other California tribe.
- Each student should read the story and the group can discuss what information was learned from the story about the tribe.
- Individuals in the group can research basic facts about the tribe. The facts should include: territory, homes, language, foods, clothing, natural resources, mission influence.
- The students will organize the story into a Reader's Theater script that they will present to the class. Students can read their parts and minimal props are needed.
- Tribal facts from group research can be shared before the presentation.

Individual Project: The student may follow the same procedure but adapt the story to share in the oral tradition.

Materials: California Indian stories, reference books, laptops, notebooks, journals, index cards, pencils, pens, any props for the presentation

Suggested California Indian stories:
Coyote and the Grasshoppers: A Pomo Legend, Gloria Dominic
Fire Race: A Karuk Coyote Tale, retold by Jonathan London
Native Ways, California Indian Stories and Memories, Malcolm Margolin
A Story of Seven Sisters, A Tongva Pleides Legend, Pamela Marx
When the Animals Were People, Kay Sanger
Two Bear Cubs, A Miwok Legend, retold by Robert D. San Souci
The Beginning of the Chumash, retold by Monique Sonoquie
The Rainbow Bridge, Audrey Wood
The Sugar Bear Story, Mary J. Yee

Recording History (Standard 4.2.3)

Primary sources are important resources to use when researching the past. In this activity the student will imagine that he is living in the 1700's and has been sent on one of the Spanish expeditions to record the progress of the missions and the sights and sounds of California.

Individual Journal Project: The student will:
- write journal entries, using appropriate dates, describing what he sees, eats, how he travels, his impressions of the missions, and the people he meets.
- describe the relationships among the soldiers, missionaries, and Indians.
- include drawings of native plants, animals, and other new natural resources that would be seen.
- use previous knowledge and new research to complete the project.

Materials: Journals, pencils, pens, colored pencils, laptops, resource books

Group Timeline Project: The students will:
- create a timeline from pre-mission to post-mission periods.
- use resources to research important facts and dates to post on the timeline.
- use drawings, photos, or other pictures to illustrate the timeline.
- display the timeline in the classroom.

Materials: Butcher paper, colored pencils, pens, paints, laptops, resource books

The Land (Standard 4.2.4)

The respect that the native people in <u>Lands of Our Ancestors</u> have for the land includes knowledge of the geography of their territory.

Group or Individual Project: The student will use the information from the story to draw a map of where the Chumash people from the Place of River Turtles built their village and the surrounding area. The map should include:
- the village
- the mission
- Sacred Mountain
- Shrine Mountain
- Mother Oak
- hunting area
- old camp
- animal trails
- river
- Pacific Ocean
- foothills
- the village where the runaway natives live
- nearby missions

Materials: Large construction paper or butcher paper, pens, colored pencils, paints, copy of story

Fact Box (Standard 4.2.5)

Group or Individual Project: This game activity reinforces new material learned in the unit of study and will motivate students to research additional information.

The student will cover and decorate a shoe box or similar size box. Decorations should illustrate one of the story themes or scenes. There should be an opening at the top of the box large enough to reach inside. Using index cards, the student will write 20 or more question cards about daily life in the missions for native and non-native people. Answers to the questions should be written on the back of the question cards. Questions can be true or false.
Examples:
Q: Who made the adobe bricks for the mission buildings?
A: The native men and boys made the adobe bricks.

Q: True or False? Native families were allowed to stay together and speak their native languages in the missions.
A: False

Students can play the game individually or in teams, taking turns choosing cards from the box. Students can decide if they want to keep score; awarding points for correct answers.

Materials: Shoe box, paper, scissors, tape, pencils, pens, crayons, index cards, laptop, resource books, copy of story

Compare and Contrast (Standard 4.2.5)

Group or Individual Project: Students will make three posters to be displayed side by side. Each poster will represent a different group; natives, priests, and soldiers living at the mission. Students will use words and pictures to illustrate each group's daily life. The side by side display will illustrate the contrast. This project can include an oral presentation or explanation of the information in the posters and students' opinions.

Materials: Poster board, pens, pencils, drawings or pictures, glue, laptop, resource books, copy of story

Native Plants (Standard 4.2.6)

Native people have always had great knowledge of plants; an important natural resource. Plants are used for food, medicine, and a variety of items ranging from cordage to sleeping mats to houses. Today, in modern times, native plants are being grown in yards and public spaces because they are drought tolerant. Native plants are also currently studied for their value in modern medicine.

Group or Individual Project: The student will choose at least four native plants used by Indians in California. The student will research the importance of the plants to the native people, the uses of the plants, where the plants grow, and any other interesting or important information. The student will research how the native plants are used today. (See plant list below.)
The student will assemble the information in a booklet or poster. Pictures of the plants should be included. The completed project can be shared with the class and displayed. Alternate display: collage of plants and information.

If space allows, students can plan and plant a native garden on school grounds or in planters.

Materials: paper, journals, poster board, pens, pencils, crayons, laptops, native plant resource books, plant pictures

Native Plant Concentration Game (Standard 4.2.6)

Group or Individual Project: Student will write the names of at least ten native plant names on index cards of one color. Then the student will write the uses of the ten native plants on index cards of a different color. Cards can be decorated.
To play the game: Shuffle the cards in both groups and match the name of the card with the use. Students can play in pairs. Students may invent other versions of the game.

Suggested native plants: willow, juncus, oak, elderberry, deergrass, yucca, agave, tule reeds, sage, milkweed, sumac, yerba mansa, soap root, manzanita, toyon.

Materials: colored index cards, pencils, crayons, native plant resource books, laptop

CPSIA information can be obtained
at www.ICGtesting.com
Printed in the USA
BVOW04s2154101017
497322BV00009B/82/P